Natures Young Readers

Animal Life

Florence Bass

PREFACE.

The subjects of this series of lessons are mainly insects or other animals as the children may observe for themselves.

The main feature of the book is its method of presenting natural science to children.

The forces of nature are personified and each object of nature studied is placed in its proper relation to its environment, thus making a story that is enjoyable not only to small children, but to those "grown-ups."

Many of the lessons aim to give only a particular instance of a general truth, to lead children to discover for themselves other like instances and finally to infer the truth itself.

The lessons aim to give illustrations of some of the varied means of self-protection employed by animals; their methods of homebuilding and of caring for their young; the transformations they undergo; the adaptability to their surroundings as shown by their coverings and the "tools" with which the various animals are provided.

The purpose in attempting to bring these thoughts to the youngest readers is manifold.

It is hoped that such readers may become interested, while children, in the abundant life about them, and that when this interest is gratified by learning of the wonderful lives and habits of these "little people," respect for all life may be inculcated.

It is desirable that children acquire such feeling for lives weaker than their own, that they may never give unnecessary pain to any creature and never take a life except in self-defense or for some other very good reasons. A child thus trained to feel for the lower forms of life cannot fail to be more considerate of his kind.

By interesting children in the wonderful ways of insects, it is hoped that the timid, fearful children, who scream if a "bug" happens to come near them, may become less fearful and find pleasure where they once found only pain. Let them learn that in most cases these insects will do them no harm, if unmolested. Let the children see that it is possible for us to learn much about insects or animals without hurting, or even touching them.

The purpose is to discourage the study of any animal at the cost of its life, or of giving it pain. If the animal cannot be kept in the school-room with a home and comforts reasonably like its own, it should not be kept at all. The children may be led to a search and observe it in its natural environment. That is the place to study life.

Leave the collecting and pulling to pieces and naming of parts to older and more scientific people, if such work must be done. Do not ask it of the tender-hearted little children, and do not countenance it in the children more cruel by nature. All knowledge that children gain by taking life or giving pain to beings weaker than themselves, seems to me to be gained at the expense of their moral nature, and is, therefore, better done without.

Finally, it is surely impossible to become acquainted, even in a slight degree, with these expressions of the wondrous thoughts of God, without being drawn nearer to their Maker and ours.

TO THE CHILDREN.

Dear LittLe Friends:

Some time ago I wrote you some little stories about plants.

I tried to show you how all plant mothers have the same thing to do: they make seeds.

These are really little cradles in which baby plants are wrapped up.

Food is left in the seed for them to eat when they begin to grow.

I also tried to let you see some of the ways the plant has to keep her seed babies from harm till they are grown.

Sometimes it is done with thorns or briers or hard shells or bitter fruit.

We saw, too, that many of them have ways of sending their little ones out into the world.

Now I wish to tell you a few things about animals.

You will see that an animal mother must also provide for her little ones.

Sometimes she has no more to do than the plant mother.

She leaves her eggs where the little ones will find food when they begin to grow.

But you may be sure she will do that much.

Sometimes she takes care of them till they are grown.

Sometimes she even gives her life for them.

In these little stories we will read some of the many ways animal mothers do these things.

As you take your walks, into the country, look about you to see how many little stories you may see acted out, for yourself.

Plants told us many things by what they did.

Now because animals can act so much more, they can tell us more.

Perhaps they really do have a way of talking to one another. They often act as if they did.

As you watch these little insects you may see them treat one another in a way that seems very cruel to you.

Suppose you watch to see why they do these things.

See if you find one animal taking the life of another except for food, or to defend itself or its home from harm.

We do that ourselves. I hope we do not do more.

When we learn so many wonderful things about these "little people" about us, they seem almost like fairies, do they not?

Remember that you are a giant in this fairyland.

I hope you will try to be a gentle giant.

Do not harm them, if you can help it.

Enjoy them by looking at them, just as you do the bright sunshine, the blue hills, and the golden sunset and every other beautiful thing in this great world of ours.

Your friend,

Florence Bass.

CONTENTS

A Little Mother	11
The Little Children	13
Wasp & Co.	14
A Digger Wasp	18
Story Of A Spider	20
In A Flower	25
Up In A Balloon	26
A Mother Spider	28
A Bridge Builder	30
Down In The Water	31
Down In The Ground	33
Evening Chorus	35
Are They Faires?	36
Honey Bees	39
The Story Of A Locust, Or Harvest Fly	42
A Basket Maker	46
A Little Builder	48
A Mosquito	50
A House Fly	53
Some Friends Of Ours	55
A Leaf-cutter Bee	59
A Butterfly	62
A Queer House	65

More About The Round House	68
A Grasshopper	68
Asleep On The Trees	71
Asleep In The Ground	73
An Owl	75
Beaver And Squirrel	76
The Duck And The Hen	80
Which Has The Best Coat?	82
A Cuttlefish	85
Some Little Dressmakers	87
Awake	89
A Cocoon	92
The Moth	93
A Kingbird	94
The Robin's Song	96
An Ant's Story	98
The Best Jumper	102
A May Fly	104
Some Little Helpers	106
Tumble Bugs	108
A Little Carpenter	110
A Queer Fellow	112
A Lady Bug's Talk	113

A Little Actor	116
A Little Gymnast	118
A Living Light	120
A Little Messenger	122
A Little Gardener	125
A Humming Bird	127
A Hawk Moth	128
A Snail	131
A Dragon	133
A Careful Little Mother	136
The Most Wonderful Of All	138

Natures Stories For Young Readers

A LITTLE MOTHER.

Children, did you ever think how much your mothers do for you?

They give you good things to eat, clothes to wear, and help to make a pleasant home for you.

Let us look at some of the very "little people" about us.

See how these little mothers take care of their little ones.

Here is a picture of a little mother.

She is Mrs. Mud Wasp. She is working very hard.

She seems to never stop for a minute.

What can she be doing?

Just now she is building her house.

See her come with a little ball of mud.

Watch her spread out this mud with her jaws.

She begins in the middle and spreads it down one side.

Now see her dart away. She has gone for more soft mud.

Soon she comes back with another piece.

She begins at the top and spreads it out on the other side.

What a noise she makes as she works!

Soon she will have one room done.

Then she goes in and leaves a little egg.

Now she must find something for her baby to eat, when it creeps out of that egg.

What do you suppose she gets? Why! Little spiders!

I have seen as many as eight spiders put in for one baby wasp to eat.

Perhaps it likes them as well as you and I like fried chicken, which our mothers get for us.

Mother Wasp walls up these spiders in a room with her egg.

Perhaps she makes many more rooms like this.

Then she flies away and never comes back.

She never sees her own little ones.

Perhaps she knows that she has taken all the care of them that they need.

THE LITTLE CHILDREN.

Would you like to know what goes on inside this mud house? I will tell you about it.

A tiny white grub creeps out of each of those eggs. It looks like a little worm.

"What!" you say, "a worm out of a wasp's egg!"

Yes, that is just what a baby wasp looks like.

It eats the spiders Mrs. Wasp left for it.

It grows bigger very fast.

I fear it does not know how hard its mother worked to get all that food for it and make its house.

After a while, it goes to sleep in a little case.

It seems to be dead, but it is not.

It is only growing to be a wasp like its mother.

By and by it wakes up,—a full-grown wasp.

It never grows anymore.

It bites a hole through its mud house and flies away.

Do you think it knows yet how much its mother did for it?

We cannot tell that.

It surely knows how to do the same things for its own little ones.

WASP & CO.

OLDEST PAPER MAKERS IN THE WORLD.

See this paper house.

It belongs to Mrs. Wasp. She is a cousin (

She makes a much finer house than her (

Her house is all made of paper.

Where do you suppose she got the paper? Can you guess?

Why! She made it herself— every bit of it.

Her folks knew how to make paper long before men did.

She picks little pieces off of old fence rails. She bites them up fine and makes them into paper.

But I must tell you the story of Mrs. Wasp and her house.

Then you will see what a wise little being she is.

She did not have this pretty house to live in last winter.

She slept in a little crack in the barn.

It was very hard to keep from freezing.

She did not need to come out to get anything to eat.

When the warm spring days came, she woke up and crept out.

She was all alone in the world.

She started out bravely to make a home of her own. She soon found a good place.

She began several rooms at once.

She makes her house in a queer way.

She begins at the top and works down.

Then her rooms are open at the bottom.

They seem the wrong side up to us.

When these little rooms were ready, she put an egg into each one.

But she did not put in anything for her baby to eat, as Mrs. Mud Wasp does.

Do not think she fails to care for her little ones.

After a while, a little grub comes out of each egg. You would think she would not own that for her baby. But she does.

Then how she must work to find food for her little ones.

She has to feed them as much as a mother bird feeds her babies.

Off goes Mrs. Wasp perhaps to the butchers. Back she comes with a fly.

Off again, here and there she flies.

She is very busy taking care of her family.

By and by you will find a little white door shutting up each room.

Mrs. Wasp does not feed the little ones now..

They are asleep. She is not uneasy about them.

Do you suppose she knows what is going on inside of those rooms?

Each little worm is turning into a wasp like its mother.

Has she not been a good little mother to them?

See what pretty rooms she made.

How carefully she fed them!

She is not afraid to fight for them, too. You will find this out if you bother her at her work.

I do not blame her for fighting for her home and children, do you?

At last, the white doors open.

Outcome the children, — full-grown worker wasps.

Now, what do you suppose these children do?

Just what all good children should do.

They go to work to help their mother.

They help build more rooms.

They clean up their old rooms for little new wasps. They help feed all the little ones.

Now Mrs. Wasp has not so much work to do.

Are you not glad she has such good children to help her?

They seem to me to be a pretty good and wise family. Do you not think so?

A DIGGER WASP.

Who is this? What is she doing?

See her digging in the dirt with her front feet, like a dog.

She is making a hole in the ground.

Can she be hunting for something to eat? Let us watch and see what she does.

Now her hole has grown quite deep.

She must go down and bring up each piece of dirt,—just as an ant does.

Now she seems to have finished her work. She takes a little piece of dirt and stops up the hole.

Off she flies, and we wait for her return.

What is she about now? I will tell you.

She has gone to get dinner ready.

Did you say, "Dinner? for whom, and of what kind?"

Why! dinner for her little one, of course.

It is going to live in that room she has made.

She means to bring back a big fat caterpillar for its dinner. I suppose she knows what is best for it.

That is all the care she has to take of it.

The food she brings will last until it turns into a wasp like its mother.

Then it can take care of itself.

Mrs. Wasp, you are not as good a house builder as your cousin Mud Wasp.

She really builds her house. You only dig into the ground.

But perhaps you do the best you know.

But Mrs. Wasp is gone for a long time.

Perhaps she is having some trouble to find her fresh meat.

I think we will not wait for her return.

STORY OF A SPIDER.

One day Mrs. Spider sat in the middle of her web.

She had on a gold and black dress.

She had a silver-gray bonnet.

She wears four pairs of stockings, you know.

They are all orange and black.

She was almost as pretty as the flowers.

What a beautiful web she had, too!

It was made of the finest silk.

It was all Mrs. Spider's own work. You must know she is the very finest of spinners.

She made a little white winding stair up one side of her web.

Then everything was all ready; so she sat down to wait for a caller.

Pretty soon a man came along.

But Mrs. Spider did not wish to see him.

So she shook her web as hard as she could.

Perhaps she thought that would keep him from seeing her.

She feared the man would kill her.

I am afraid he would, too; though I cannot see why he should.

He does not seem to know that she is one of his best friends.

But so she is; she is a benefit to him every day.

She eats insects that are harmful to him or his garden.

But she herself does him no harm.

Pretty soon the man went away.

Then Mrs. Spider sat quite still again.

Ah! who is this flying so swiftly toward the spider web?

It is Mrs. Mud Wasp.

Is she the caller that is wanted?

We will watch to see how she is received.

But where is Mrs. Spider?

She is not in sight.

It is quite plain that she has run off from Mrs. Mud Wasp.

It is well that she did.

If she had not, Mrs. Mud Wasp would have run off with her.

But what has become of Mrs. Spider?

She saw Mrs. Mud Wasp coming.

She knew, too, why she was coming.

Quick as a flash she dropped from her web.

She spun a line to run back upon.

Now she is lying quite still upon the ground.

Perhaps she is laughing to herself: "I beat you this time, Mrs. Mud Wasp."

If Mrs. Wasp should see her lying on the ground, she would not care to touch her.

Mrs. Spider is playing "dead" down there.

She is all curled up in a little bunch.

She knows how to keep herself safe.

Mrs. Mud Wasp does not care for a dead spider. So off she goes.

Now Mrs. Spider comes to life very quickly.

She climbs up her silken rope to her web.

Again she sits still, waiting for the right caller.

For whom can she be waiting so long?

She hopes some insect will come flying along.

If he does not see her web, he may be caught in it.

That is the only way she has to get the meat for her dinner.

You see the caller she wants is the one who brings her something for dinner. He may be here soon.

I think I will go on, Mrs. Spider.

I do not care to see you get your dinner ready.

IN A FLOWER.

Here is another little spider.

She does not build a web to catch her dinner.

Do you see what she does instead?

She hides in a flower.

You can scarcely see her, unless you look very closely.

She is very nearly the color of the flower she sits upon.

Does she know colors?

How can she tell which flower matches her dress?

She seems to know, for she never goes to one of the wrong colors.

Why is she so anxious to match the flower?

She has two reasons: First, that she may not be seen by her enemies.

They may pounce upon her and carry her off.

Then she does not wish to be seen by the little insects that come to the flower to feed. Then she can jump up and catch them for her dinner.

That is the way she has to make her living.

Ah! little fairy, who gave you that pretty dress?

Who taught you where to hide and how to get your living?

UP IN A BALLOON.

Who made the balloon?

Who is going up in it?

The same answer will do for both questions.

For it was no other than Mrs. Spider herself.

She wished to take a journey. She had no wings to fly with.

She could not go on the cars as we do.

She climbed to the top of that plant.

She stiffened out her legs and held up her body.

She spun a number of light silken threads.

They were so light they floated upward.

Soon she had spun so many, she felt they would bear her up.

So she gave a little leap, and away she sailed through the air.

Her silk threads carried her, just as the silk threads carry the milkweed seeds.

But she makes her own balloon. She can ride a long distance. If she wishes to come down, she can roll up her threads. Then her own weight will take her down.

Is she not like a fairy to do such wonderful things?

A MOTHER SPIDER.

Here is a little mother spider. See the big ball she carries with her!

Do you know what is inside?

She has hundreds of eggs in it.

She carries this ball of eggs about with her.

She will fight for it.

She will lose one of her legs rather than her egg-ball.

Is she not a brave little mother?

When the little spiders hatch out, she cares for them, too.

Sometimes they ride on her back as she goes about.

But the little spiders grow very fast.

Soon their skins are too small. They change them for new ones.

They will soon be able to care for themselves.

Their mother takes good care of them till that time.

A BRIDGE BUILDER.

Little Mrs. Spider sat upon a bush by the side of a brook.

"Now, how shall I cross?" she said to herself.

Then she thought, "Why, there must be a bridge, of course.

"There seems to be none here. I must build one myself."

So she at once began to spin.

You know what a fine spinner she is.

Her loom is always with her and ready.

Soon a soft silken line floated out into the air.

Mrs. Spider sat quite still and waited.

She knew what would likely happen.

The line floated gently over the stream and lodged in a bush beyond.

That was just what she was waiting for.

If her first line had not gone there, she would have tried again.

Now see her run over her light line.

She spins another as she goes.

At the other side, she tightens the thread.

Back and forth she goes, making her bridge stronger each

time.

And now her fairy bridge is done.

Who could find a better way to get the first line across the brook?

Spiders have built bridges this way for many years.

Once a man wished to build a bridge.

He sent a kite over a river to get the first line across.

Do you suppose Mrs. Spider made him think of that way of doing it?

DOWN IN THE WATER.

Now we must hear a story of a diver.

Strange to say, this diver has her home in the water.

Who can the diver be?

Why, another spider. She says: "I will have the safest place of all for my babies. I will build my house down under the water."

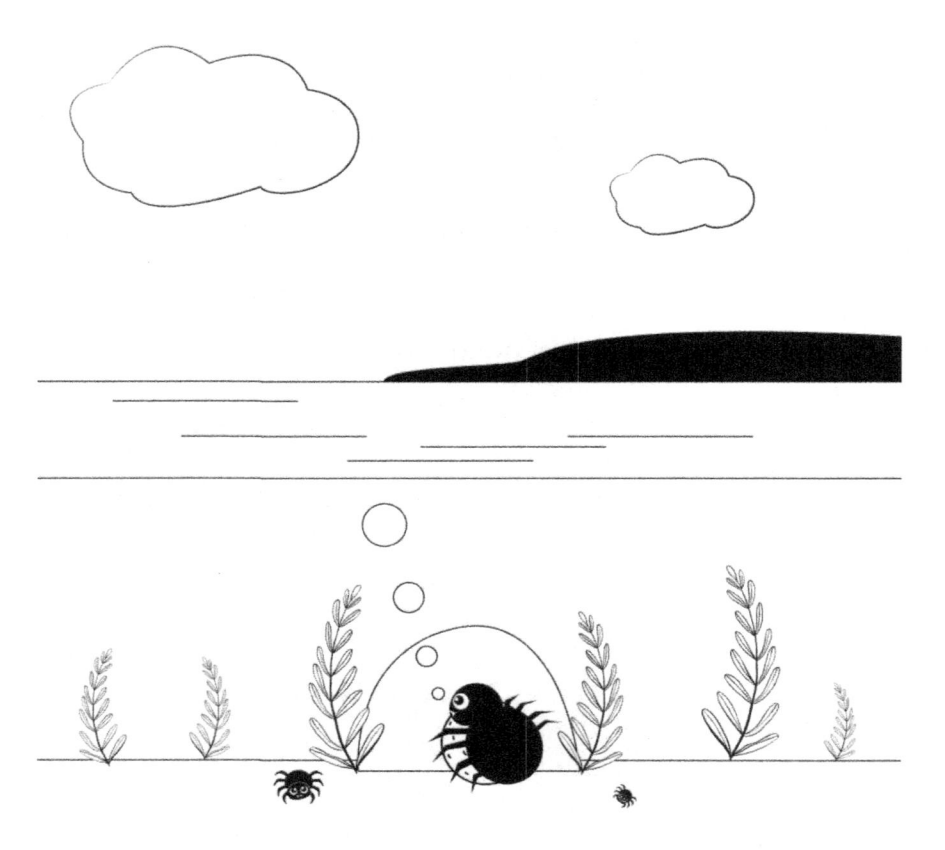

So she really does make a little silken house down there.

How can she live down in the water?

She must have air to breathe.

She really brings bubbles of air with her, and fills up her little home.

There she makes her cocoon and lays her eggs.

There she raises her baby spiders.

Is she not a queer builder?

DOWN IN THE GROUND.

Let us hear about the house of another spider.

She still has a different way of building her home.

She digs a round hole down into the earth.

But she cannot have only bare mud walls for her house.

Not she: so she works hard, as any tidy housekeeper should, to make her house look well.

She weaves the finest and most beautiful silken curtains.

She covers her walls with them.

Then she makes a door that just fits into the top of her house.

She fastens it on with a hinge.

She makes it a little larger at the top than at the bottom.

Then it cannot fall in upon her.

She covers the inside of this door with a silken curtain, too.

But it would not do to leave the outside of it mud color.

That would show everybody where she lives.

She does not wish any visitors.

Poor little thing! She knows they would not treat her well.

They might kill her and her babies.

So she covers her door outside with such plants as she sees around her.

This mother spider has a pretty safe place for her little ones.

It is very hard to find such a nest.

I think she has earned her safety.

Do you not think so?

EVENING CHORUS.

Given by the Summer Night Glee Club. Beginning August first.

Every night until frost.

Mr. Frog, Mr. Screech Owl, and Mr. Katy-Did are the soloists.

Mr. Black Cricket and the noted Tree Cricket will also be heard.

Grand orchestra of over one thousand crickets!!

The numbers on this program are selected especially to please the ladies.

Mr. Firefly will furnish calcium lights on these grand occasions!!

Music begins promptly at dusk and continues till dawn.

Do not fail to hear the music.

Admission free to all who have ears to hear!!!

ARE THEY FAIRIES?

One day I walked out into the garden.

I saw some white things flying about over the cabbage. What could they be?

Do you think they were snowflakes?

No, indeed; for it was a hot summer.

Were they little flowers?

No; for they flew about, here and there.

They looked like little fairies all dressed in white.

Ah! they were beautiful white butterflies.

What could they have been doing?

Do you think they liked cabbage to eat?

Not so; they were too dainty for such fare.

They stopped just a moment on a leaf.

Then off they darted to another.

I looked closely where one of them stopped. I found a tiny green egg.

Not long after, a little green worm crept out of the ogg.

It did not look at all like it's pretty white mother.

Such a greedy little thing as it was!

Cabbage is just what 1t wanted to eat.

That is why its mother left her egg there.

How do you suppose she knew that?

That is her way of taking care of it.

She put it where it could get plenty to eat.

The little worm ate so much that it grew very fast.

By and by it stopped eating. It seemed to grow sleepy.

A little green skin covered it all over.

It did not move, I could see neither head nor legs.

It stayed there a few days. Then it broke its shell and crept out.

It was a beautiful white butterfly like its mother.

Does this not sound like a fairy story?

And yet it is all true.

You may see all these things yourself.

You cannot see the fairy that changes the green worm to a butterfly.

But you can sec that it is done.

HONEY BEES.

See this little bee on the flower. What is she doing?

She has two baskets with her.

Do you know where they are?

She has come to market. Watch her a moment.

You will see her filling her baskets with flower dust.

See how much flower dust she already has.

What is she going to do with this dust?

She will take it home to make bee bread for the baby bees.

Do you know where her home is?

I am sure you have all seen the outside of the pretty beehive where she lives.

You have seen the busy workers going in and out.

You have seen them going to the flowers for honey.

Perhaps you have seen the drones crawling about doing nothing.

But, poor fellows! they have a hard enough time, after all.

The workers sting them to death when winter comes.

You have seen the beautiful honeycomb.

You know how it is all made of little cells or rooms.

Each has just six sides.

You have all tasted the sweet honey the 238 bees make. You know how good it is.

You do not need to be told how much the bees do for us.

Do you not wonder how they can make the honey from the flowers?

We could not do it.

If you could only go inside the bees house, what wonders you would see!

You would see the queen bee herself. She is the mother of all.

How she is petted and cared for by the others!

You would perhaps see the bees making the wax cells.

You would find bee bread in some cells.

You would find baby bees in other cells.

Perhaps you would find baby queens in some.

Ah! but there is trouble when one of them comes out!

There must not be two queens in one hive.

So the new queen and the old one fight till one kills the other.

Or a part of the workers go off with one queen and start a new home of their own.

Then we say they swarm.

Bees are very hard-working little people.

They work so hard to lay up honey for themselves.

But they make much more than they need.

So there is plenty for us.

THE STORY OF A LOCUST, OR HARVEST FLY.

Do you see that little brown shell?

I used to live there.

I will tell you about my life.

But first, you must know my name.

My real name is Cicada.

If that is too hard to say, you may call me a Harvest Fly.

I do not like to be called a Locust. I will tell you why.

Real locusts are a kind of grasshopper.

Sometimes many of them come together.

They eat up every green thing they can find.

Now, I do not do such bad things as that.

I do not eat up your crops.

I sit up in the trees these hot days and make music.

My mate likes to hear me. Do you?

A year ago, Mother Cicada put a great many little eggs into a twig.

In a few weeks, I crept out of one of those eggs.

I was very small then, — as little as an ant.

I knew that my home was to be on the ground.

But how should I get there?

I was afraid to crawl down the tree.

Something might catch me.

So I crept out to the end of the branch and let go.

Down I went, over and over, to the ground.

It did not hurt me at all.

I bored my way down into the ground.

I ate roots for my food.

I did not look as I do now.

I was only an ugly bug.

I grew to be as big as that shell.

Last week something seemed to call me up into the bright world.

So I bored my way through the ground and came out.

I crawled up on that twig you see there.

I fixed my claws into it very firmly.

Then a queer thing happened; my dry brown coat split open on the back.

I pushed my back up, and then pulled out my head. Next came out my four wings.

They were little soft green things, all crumpled up.

Then one by one I pulled out my legs.

They were very weak at first.

I leaned over backwards and moved them up and down. That made them grow stronger.

At last, I pulled my whole body out of my shell.

But I clung to it with my feet.

Then you should have seen my wings.

Larger and larger they grew.

They soon became as large as they are now.

But they were still quite soft and the veins were green.

Before long my wings were hard and glassy, and the veins were black.

I can fly now wherever I choose.

I am glad to get out of the ground into this beautiful world.

Do you wonder that I love to sit up in the trees and make music?

A BASKET MAKER.

Look what a fine basket I have made.

I live in the basket. It is really my house.

I made it around me.

Does it seem queer to you to build a house and stay inside of it all the time?

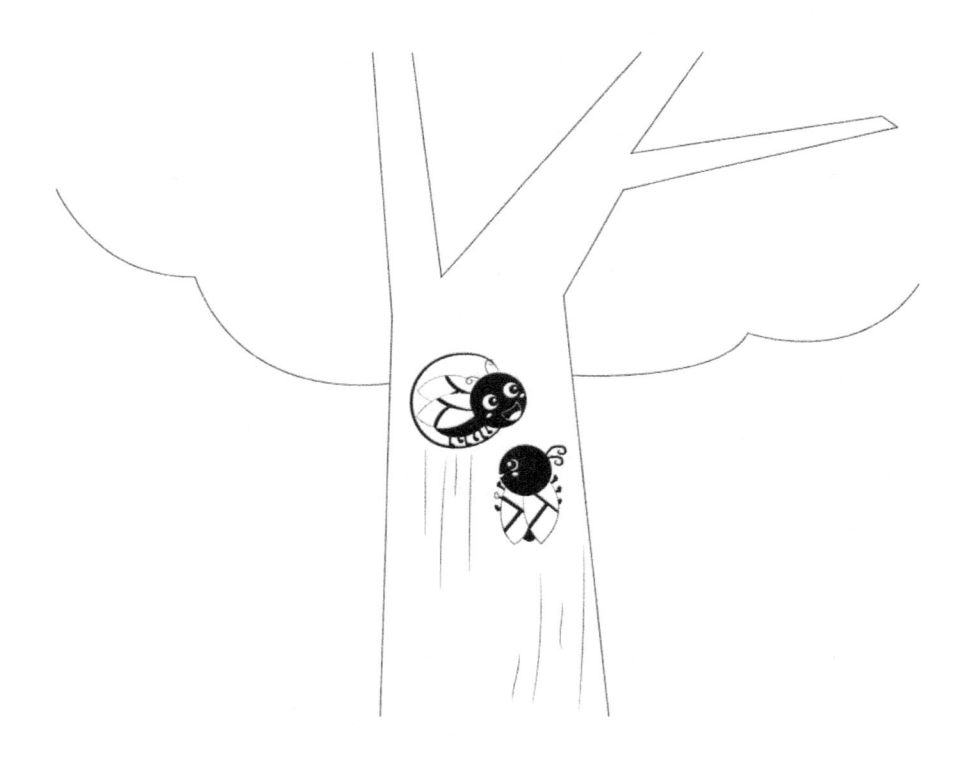

I began it when I was very little.

As I grew bigger, I kept making my house bigger.

I reach over and fasten the little pieces on the outside.

I carry my house with me, as I travel over the tree.

If I am seared, I creep inside and shut myself in.

I creep nearly out if I wish to find something to eat.

I still hold fast to my basket.

By and by I shall shut myself inside and sleep for some time.

When I wake up I can fly away; for I shall be a little moth.

My little mate never leaves her house.

She has no wings, so she cannot fly.

She lays many little eggs in her basket.

Next spring her babies will come out of them.

Then each one will begin to make a basket for himself.

He does not need to stop to learn how.

He may be on a locust or cedar or pine tree.

He does not seem to care.

He goes to work and makes the best basket he can of what he has.

Is that not a pretty good way?

A LITTLE BUILDER.

Here is a picture of a queer little house in the water.

The little builder lives inside.

He is called a Caddis Worm.

Do you see his fanny little house?

It is made of tiny shells and stones.

Mr. Caddis Worm has a very soft little body.

He could not live long in the water without his house.

A hungry fish would soon find him.

What can he do? He must find a safe place to live.

Perhaps he has seen Mr. Snail with his house on his back. He sees what a good thing that is.

But no house has been given to Mr. Caddis Worm.

Perhaps he has heard how Mr. Basket Worm has made a house for himself.

He may think: "Well, I can do that myself."

But he has a harder task than Mr. Basket Worm.

He has to build right in the water.

He picks up little shells or bits of stone, or whatever he can find.

He sticks them together with a kind of glue he makes himself.

He begins his house when he is very little.

As he grows bigger, he must keep adding to it.

He fastens a little silken door over the end of his house.

Can you guess what goes on inside of that house?

Perhaps you can if you look at the picture.

Yes, he flies away; for when he comes out, he has wings. Then he is called a Caddis Fly.

I am glad he has such pretty wings.

He worked so hard to make his house, I think he ought to have a good time now.

A MOSQUITO.

Here is an enemy of ours. She has a pretty, graceful form, but I am quite sure that none of us will ever like her.

And no wonder; she does not treat us at all well.

If only she would let us alone, then we would not bother about her so much.

We do not like her song. We do not like her bite.

So take care, Mrs. Mosquito, We must fight for ourselves

if you attack us.

Let us see if we cannot learn something of interest about her.

That is all the good we may hope to get from her, I am sure.

The rain barrel will be a good place to go to learn about her.

No, she does not live there now; she did live there once.

We will go to see how she began life.

Ah! there is a little piece of brown lint floating on the water.

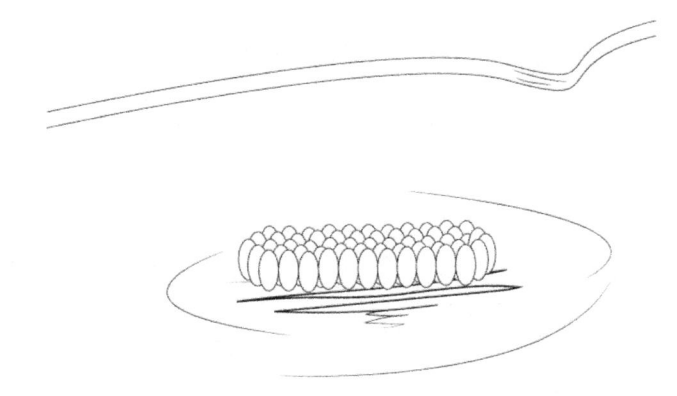

No, indeed; that is a whole boat of mosquito eggs glued together.

Is it not a queer place for Mrs. Mosquito to leave her eggs?

But she knows as what she is about, I suppose.

After a while, little wiggle-tails come out of these eggs.

Watch them as they go wriggling through the water.

How funny they are!

See those little hairs at the end of their tails.

They breathe through those hairs.

As they grow larger, they split open their skins and come out.

You often see their old skins lying on the water.

After a while, they seem to have changed.

If you shake the water, down they go tumbling over and over to the bottom.

Then they are called tumblers.

But soon the tumblers break their skins and come out, — mosquitoes.

They must be very careful while drying their wings.

They will drown if they fall into the water.

Yes, in the very place where they have lived.

Is not that queer?

Ah! there is one nearly ready to fly off and bite us. We must run or fight.

Well, you are very interesting, Mrs. Mosquito.

You may be very smart, but you are not kind, which would be better.

I do not like you.

A HOUSE FLY.

Thank you, little girl. That was very kind of you to help me out of that dish of water.

You have saved my life.

I am sure that you are kind to all things.

You did not like to see me struggling there in the water.

You were willing to help me, though you do not like me.

I would like to do something for you.

I will sit still and let you see the beautiful colors on my wings.

See how I rub my legs together.

That is the way I keep them clean.

See how quickly I can bend my head and give it a rub.

I wash somewhat as your cat does.

See my long trunk! Watch me suck up my food through it.

If you had such eyes as I have, you could see more things about me.

I have hundreds of eyes.

I do not have to turn my head as you do, when I wish to see around.

My eyes look every way.

I have wonderful little feet.

I can walk on the ceiling with my head down.

Just think of that!

We have a hard time, I can tell you.

People often wish that there were no flies in the world.

But even we do some good.

We eat up things that would make the air bad if left alone.

Qur children live on just such things.

But I must fly off now, and keep out of your house.

I will tell my friends, too, not to bother you.

You were kind to me.

SOME FRIENDS OF OURS.

I.

Here is one of them. Her name is Ichneumon Fly.

What a big, hard name! It means a "tracker."

And what a wonderful tracker she is!

No hunter or dog could find his prey better.

And why is she such a good hunter? Do you think she hunts for fun?

No, indeed; she is finding food for her little ones.

To be a true little mother she must surely do that.

She knows that her children will eat insect food only.

I cannot tell you how she knows that.

She does not eat such food herself.

She did when she was young, of course.

Do you suppose she can remember it?

Her great work in life is to find the right place to lay her eggs.

Perhaps she goes along on a tree.

She wishes to find where Mrs. Beetle left her egg and the food for her little one.

She taps and taps on the tree.

Soon she finds the place.

Outcomes her long sharp drill from its case.

She bores a hole and leaves her eggs there.

Drill and case together look only like a black hair.

Perhaps she goes to a cocoon and leaves her eggs in it.

Then after a while, her children will come out of it instead of a moth or a butterfly.

II.

Here is another Ichneumon Fly.

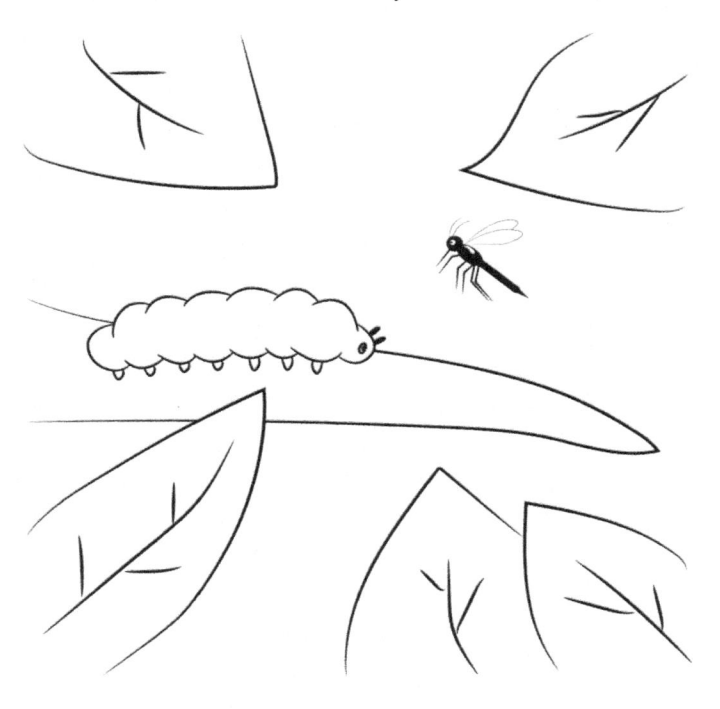

See how tiny she is.

She will never grow any bigger.

Perhaps you think she is too little to be of any use. Let us see.

She knows that her little ones will need the body of a caterpillar for food.

So that is the very place she leaves her eggs.

By and by the little ones come out of these eggs.

Soon they spin tiny white cocoons for themselves.

You may often see these little white cocoons all over a caterpillar's body.

Before long little white lids will open, and tiny ichneumons will fly out.

I called the ichneumon flies our friends.

Of course, they do not know they are of any use to us.

They go about their own work in the best way they know.

In doing that they help rid our garden of many things that are harmful to it.

A LEAF-CUTTER BEE.

One day I saw a tiny hole in the plowed ground.

Soon a little bee alighted near it.

She had a little piece of a leaf folded up between her hind legs.

She crept into the hole with it.

I could not see what she did inside.

Soon she came out and flew away.

In a little while, she came back with another leaf.

The pieces of leaves were nearly round.

Is it not queer that she can cut them out herself?

She carries her scissors with her.

She knows how to make a circle.

I watched her for some time. She seemed to be working very hard.

After several days I went back.

The bee had gone away. I waited some time, but she did not come back.

I thought I would like to see what she had done.

I saw a man coming with a plow.

In another minute her nest would be plowed up.

So I dug down into the ground and found her nest,

It looked like a little roll of leaves.

Each leaf had been cut just the right shape by the little bee.

The leaves on the sides were long.

A leaf was laid over the place where two others came together.

At the ends were the round pieces of leaves.

There were more than thirty pieces in this nest.

Yet this nest was not as large as they are sometimes.

I began to unroll the little bundle.

I was anxious to see what I should find inside.

At last, I had taken off all the leaves.

There was one tiny white grub, and a great deal of bee bread.

Mrs. Bee knows how to make bee bread out of the yellow flower dust.

You think that was a great deal of dinner to put up for such a little being.

But remember that it grows very much bigger eating all that food.

She put up enough to last till it was ready to go to sleep and change into a bee.

Then it could come out and take care of itself as its mother did.

A BUTTERFLY.

How do you do, my little friend?

I am glad you stopped there on that flower.

I have followed you for some time.

Oh! do not be afraid. I will not hurt you.

I do not wish to catch you.

Why should I do that?

You would not look pretty, then.

I could not bear to hold you fast, and have you trying to get away from me.

I only wish to look at you.

How pretty you look, flitting there over the flower.

How beautiful your wings look as you close and open them!

Why are you sitting there? Are you getting your dinner?

You must be very dainty to eat only what you find there.

What a long tongue you have! It looks like a black thread.

I love to see you unroll it and put it down into the flower.

How queer it looks to see you roll it up like a watch spring. Do you always roll it up when you are not using it?

Do you remember when you were a caterpillar?

What a greedy thing you were then!

How you did eat and eat!

I am glad you have more dainty ways now.

And you have such pretty wings!

What! Must you be going, Mr. Butterfly?

I am glad you did not fly off at first, when I came up so close to see you.

I hope to see you again.

A QUEER HOUSE.

What is this?

It grew on an oak tree; but it is not an acorn.

It is a little round house.

It has no doors or windows.

How can anyone get in or out?

Noone can get in very well.

But someone will come out, by and by.

How do you suppose he ever got in?

He grew up there. His house grew, too.

Is that not queer?

Let us hear about it.

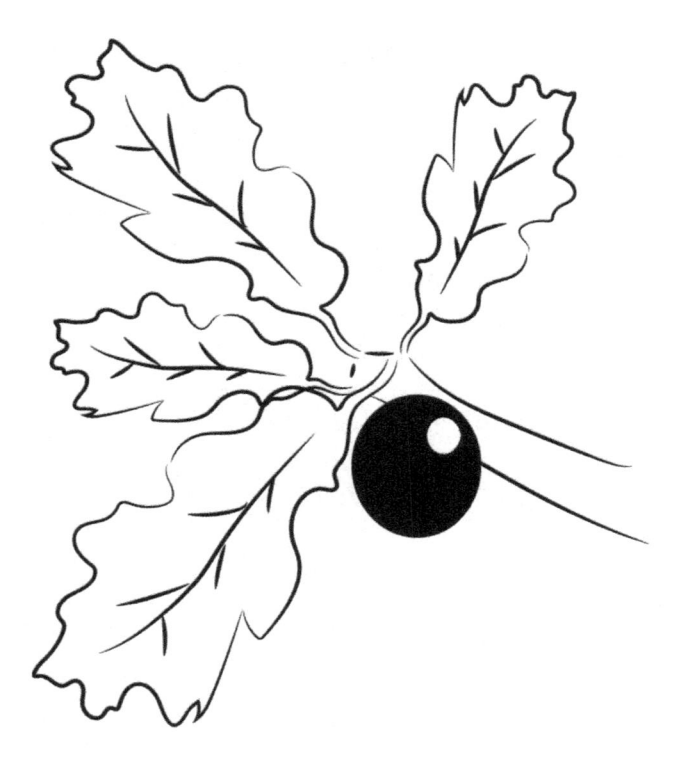

One day a gall-fly came up to the place where this house is now.

She took out her sharp drill from its case.

She made a hole with it.

Inside the hole, she put an egg.

She must have put in something else to make this house grow.

In a short time, there was the little round house, just as you see it.

By and by a little grub will come out of the egg.

He will begin at once to eat his house.

Do you not think that is funny?

But it is just what he needs for food.

See how handy that is for him!

He does not have to come out to hunt for his dinner.

After a while, he has eaten enough.

He goes to sleep and changes into a gall-fly like his mother.

He is ready to come out into the world.

He has lived shut up in his castle long enough.

Oh, if he only had his front door open!

But that does not worry him.

He has never been out into the world; but he knows just what to do.

He cuts his way through his house.

Off he flies and leaves his front door open.

He is done with his house now.

Does this not sound like a fairy story?

Isn't the round house like an enchanted fairy palace?

MORE ABOUT THE ROUND HOUSE.

I have another queer thing to tell you about the round house.

I must tell you what such houses are to us.

"What!" you say; "how can we use them?

"They are not good to eat. They are too little for us to live in."

But stop,—we make something from them.

There is something in them that helps to make good black ink.

Just think of that! Perhaps the ink I am using now was made of just such fairy houses!

You see the little fairy builder does some good for us, too, with her magic wand.

A GRASSHOPPER.

How do you do, Mr. Grasshopper?

What very long legs you have!

Yes, they help me to jump. But I can fly, too.

Did you ever see my wings?

As I sit still here, you cannot see them. They are all folded up like a fan.

I have long straight wing covers to keep them safe.

Watch me when I fly. Then you will see what big fine wings I have.

They are nearly as pretty as a butterfly's wings.

But I am not like a butterfly.

I never was an ugly crawling worm.

When I was young, I looked nearly as I do now.

But I was very little and I had no wings.

As I grew bigger, of course, I out-grew my first coat.

I had nobody to make me a new suit as you have.

My old coat was so little, I split it open down the back; but no one said a word to me for that.

That is the way I take my coat off.

Now comes the best part of my story.

As soon as my old coat was off, there was a new one already made.

It was on me, too, and fit me exactly.

Whenever I outgrow my old coat, I take it off.

I always find a new one under it ready-made.

My wings have been growing ever since I was little. But they are grown now.

I am grown, too. I shall not need to change my coat anymore.

This one will not wear out, nor will I outgrow it.

I have everything now that I need.

ASLEEP ON THE TREES.

Look at the bare trees.

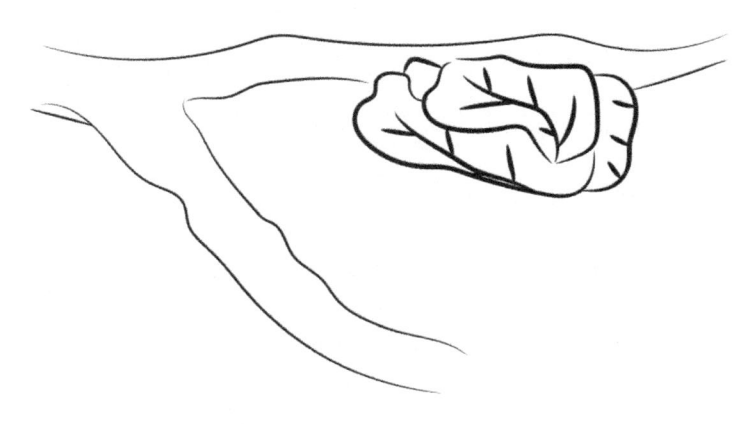

But what is this on a twig? Can it be a bud?

No, it is too big for a bud.

It is a big brown cradle.

The little sleeper inside made his own cradle. You should have seen him do it!

Spin, spin, spin! How hard he did work!

When his cradle was done, he went to sleep.

Do you know what he was?

Only a big green caterpillar.

Next spring the warm sun will waken him.

He will creep out of his cradle.

He will not have to crawl anymore.

He will be a beautiful moth.

I hope you will see him.

Here is a branch with a few leaves still hanging upon it.

Why do they still hang to the tree?

Go close and look.

Strange sight! They are tied to the tree with silk.

Who could have done such a thing?

The little fellow inside of the leaf did it.

Did he know that leaves fall off before winter comes?

Did he wish to be sure that his bed would still swing on the tree-top?

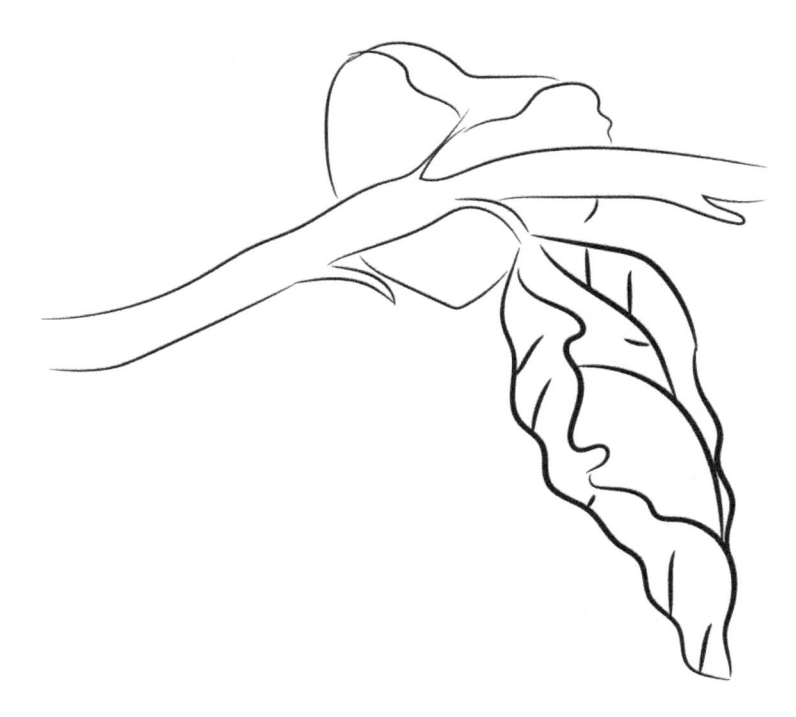

At any rate, he has tied his leaf fast to the twig. And he has gone inside for his long sleep.

He went in a caterpillar; he will come out a moth.

All winter long he will sleep in his cradle on the tree-top.

No fear has him of wind or storm.

He is only waiting for the soft spring air to wake him.

ASLEEP IN THE GROUND.

How hard and bare the earth looks!

Now we see no ants crawling about.

No grasshopper flies off as we walk.

Not many living things greet us, as they did in the summer. What has become of them? Are they dead?

The ants are down in their home in the ground.

The frogs have hidden in the mud, to sleep all winter.

Many caterpillars sleep in their cocoons in the ground.

Some spiders have hidden inside of dead leaves on the ground.

Crickets and grasshoppers have left their eggs m the ground.

Here and there, under logs or stones or in cracks, wasps and bumblebees and others have hidden.

In their hives, the honey-bees spend their winter.

They have plenty of sweet honey to eat.

As we go about this bleak wintry weather, it seems as if nearly all life were gone.

But it only sleeps in bud and seed, in egg and cocoon, in earth and water.

The Giver of life can wake it in the morning of the year.

AN OWL

One day a boy and his father went hunting.

The boy sat down on the log to rest.

Pretty soon his father came up,

"Why, my son," he said, "see that owl!"

"Where?" said the boy.

"On the log near you."

There sat the owl almost near enough for the boy to touch it. And he had not seen it.

Can you think why?

I will tell you.

Mr. Owl sat very still. He did not move.

His feathers were against the log.

He was nearly the same color as the log, so that he looked like a part of it.

He did not open his big eyes.

He only peeped through one eye, to see what the boy was doing.

He did not get scared and jump off.

He seemed to think if he gat very still, the boy would not see him.

Was not that a cute idea of his?

That was his way of protecting himself from harm.

He is a pretty wise old fellow, is he not?

BEAVER AND SQUIRREL.

"Good morning, little squirrel; may I ask what you are doing?"

"Certainly, Mr. Beaver; I am working very hard to lay up my winter store of nuts."

"How do you get your nuts cracked? You are so little, you surely cannot do it."

"Yes, I can; I do it with my sharp teeth.

"Watch me as I turn a nut over and over in my sharp claws and gnaw it.

"My teeth wear away as I use them.

"That keeps them sharp.

"They keep growing all the time, so that they do not wear out."

"Why," said the beaver, "I have just such teeth as that myself.

"But I can gnaw much bigger flings than nuts with my teeth. I can gnaw down a tree."

"Indeed! but why should you do that?"

"We need the trees to make a dam across the water.

"Come with me, someday, and I will show you how we do it.

"Many of us work together in winter. We can work better in that way.

"We make ourselves houses to live in. They are made of sticks, and plastered over with mud."

"How do you plaster them?" said the squirrel.

"We do it with our big flat tails. They are our trowels."

"Is that why you have such queer flat tails?"

"Yes, that is it. We could not work very well if we had such long hairy tails as yours.

"Your tail is beautiful, but does you no good, I fear."

"There you are mistaken! It is so light that it bears me up, when I leap from one part of the tree to another."

"I must tell you more about what we can build," said the beaver.

"We like to have the water come up over our front door. We are safer then.

"Sometimes the water does not come up high enough.

"Then we must build a dam to make it rise higher.

"We cut down all the trees we need.

"We build the dam of trees and sticks and stones, and plaster it with mud."

"How do you get into your house if the water comes over the front door?"

"We swim to it. Our hind feet are webbed, so they make good paddles for swimming.

"I see you have sharp claws, little squirrel.

"What are they for?"

"They help me to cling to the tree as I climb up."

"We are not much alike, surely.

"But each of us seems to have the things he most needs."

THE DUCK AND THE HEN.

"Good morning, Mrs. Hen," quacked the duck.

"Good morning," clucked the hen.

"Let us take a walk," said the duck.

"Very well, friend Duck, I shall be glad to go with you. I enjoy a good walk. I always find so many good things to eat on the way."

"Let us go down to the pond and have a good swim."

"Swim!" said the hen. "Not I!

I do not enjoy having my dress so wet and drabbled.

"Why, I run in out of the rain whenever I can.

"I look like a fright with my dress wet. It makes me cross, too. No, no; you do not catch me going into the water."

"Well, this is queer," said the duck.

"Now, I love to go into the water, whenever I can.

"It does not get my dress wet at all.

"The rain slips right off of my back.

"But if you cannot swim, you can run much better than I can.

"The children all laugh when they see me running. They say I waddle. Perhaps I do. '

"That is because my legs are set so far back on my body. I can swim better with them so."

"O, Mrs. Duek, let us stop here and scratch a bit! I am sure you will find a nice lunch."

"Well, now, that is something that I cannot do.

"Just look at my feet! Do you see the web between my toes? No, no; I cannot scratch.

"I'll just take a dip into the pond.

"I shall put my broad, flat bill down into the mud to find

my lunch."

"I am afraid my sharp bill would do very little good in the mud," said the hen.

"I'll just scratch here till you come back.

"Then we shall go home together."

WHICH HAS THE BEST COAT?

I.

Look first at the fish's coat.

It is made of hard, shiny scales.

The scales lap over so as to keep the water out.

They are hard so that they cannot become soaked with water.

That would make them heavy.

They are only so that the fish can slip easily through the water.

They are in many pieces so that his body can bend easily in swimming.

How could he have a better coat?

II.

Now we will look at the bird's coat.

How beautiful it is, all made of feathers!

How soft and light they are!

They will not be heavy for her to carry as she flies up.

Indeed, they help her to fly.

See how wide she can spread out her wings.

She can press on a great deal of air with them.

That is what makes her rise.

Ah! what a good coat she has!

III.

Here is an animal who has another kind of coat.

It is very thick and very hard.

It is all in two pieces.

It will open like a book.

Mr. Mussel lives inside.

How can he get about with such a heavy coat?

But stop! he does not need to get about much.

He lives in the water. The waves bring his food to him.

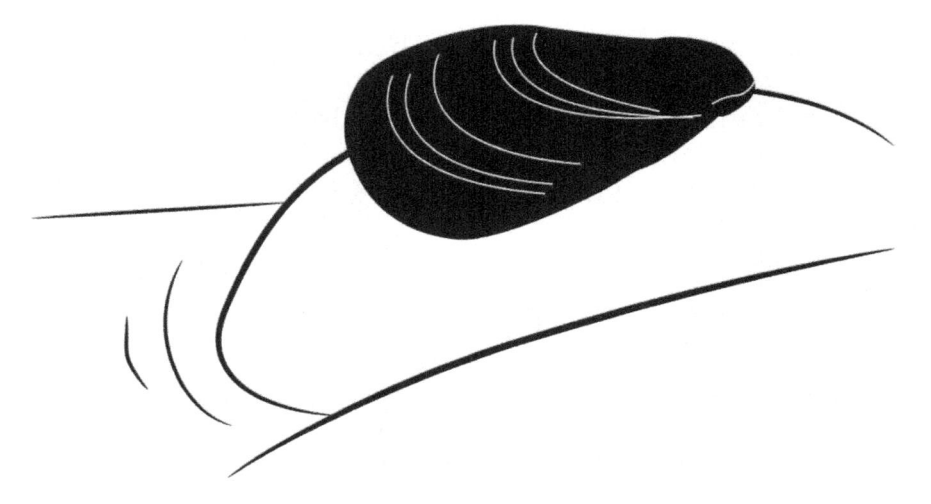

He needs only to open his shell and take it in.

His coat is so hard because his body is so very soft. He needs something hard upon it to keep him from harm.

Suppose he lived in the water and had the coat of a bird, what would become of him?

Suppose the bird had his or the fish's coat, what could she do?

Each one seems to have what is best for his own use.

A CUTTLEFISH.

A big fish was swimming about in the sea in search of food.

He soon spied a cuttlefish.

"Ah?" said Mr. Big Fish, "now I shall have a good dinner."

So he swam after Mr. Cuttlefish as fast as he could.

On swam the little fish pretty fast also.

Suddenly the water seemed to become quite black.

"Why!" said Mr. Big Fish, "what can be the matter? What has become of my dinner?

"I cannot see anything!

"Has it suddenly become night, or have I gone blind?"

So he swam around as best he could.

Soon he got into the clear water again.

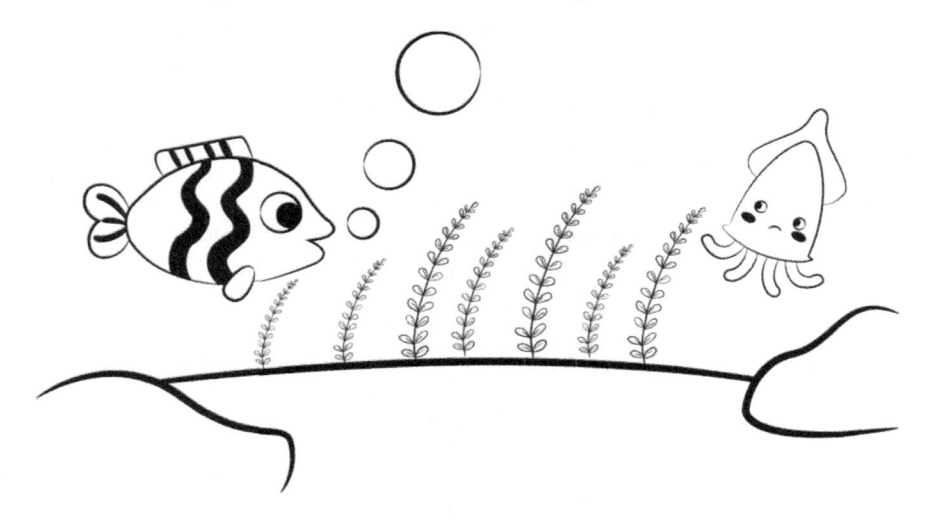

There all was as light and bright as before.

But what had become of Mr. Cuttle fish?

Shall I tell you a secret that Mr. Big Fish did not know?

Mr. Cuttlefish always carries an ink-bag with him.

He saw that the big fish was about to catch him.

So he emptied his bag into the water.

That made the water black all about him.

Then Mr. Big Fish could not see him.

So you see he could easily swim off another way.

Is not that a pretty good way of saving himself from harm?

SOME LITTLE DRESSMAKERS.

Ah! see this pretty wool dress!

Look at the holes in it.

Some dresses have been cut out of it.

The dressmakers were only little moths.

How do you suppose they got into this dress?

They have lived there all their lives. Their mother flew into the closet sometime when the door was open.

Or perhaps she crept through the keyhole.

She laid her eggs in several places.

Little things that looked like worms came out of these eggs.

Their mother did not stay to take care of them.

She knew they could take care of themselves.

She needed only to leave them on this dress.

The little moths at once began to make themselves dresses out of this one.

They bit out the pieces and wove them together.

They made themselves nice little cases or dresses.

By and by they grew too big for their little dresses.

What did they do then?

Why! the most sensible thing in the world.

They cut open their old dresses and set in a new piece.

That made them bigger, you see.

They did this as often as they grew too big for the old dresses.

Can you guess what they had to eat all this time?

Why! this dress, to be sure!

After a while, they will shut themselves up in these cases.

They will sleep till they are ready to come out with wings.

They will be ready to lay eggs in someone's clothing. They must provide for their own baby moths.

That is their way of doing it.

Well, little moths, you are pretty cunning little dressmakers. But I am not willing to let you make your dresses out of mine.

I mean to keep you out of my closet.

AWAKE.

The gentle South Wind has come again.

He says: "Go back, cold North Wind, to your home. You have played your rough pranks long enough.

"You have had your time playing with the ice and snow.

"The Spring Sun and April Rain and I must have our time

now.

"All the little people in the big brown house have been asleep all winter.

"We mean to call them up.

"The Sun makes the big room warm.

"The Ram taps gently on their doors.

"I call softly: 'Wake up, little people, your long winter sleep is over.

"Come, little ants, you may begin your work now.

"Wake up, Mr. Frog, and creep out of your mud house.

"Come, little bees; the flowers are getting your breakfast ready.

"They will soon be calling you to come and help them at seed-making.

"Come, butterflies and moths; creep out of your cradles on the tree-tops and in the ground.

"Make the country more beautiful, you are flying flowers."

Watch how gladly all the little people obey the South Wind.

At the first call, many of them peep from their hiding places.

Some of them can scarcely wait to be called.

At the first hint of a warm day, they peep out, hoping it is time to get up.

But often the cold sends them back to bed again.

But now the South Wind and the Sun have sent Jack Frost and North Wind off for a long time.

So the little people are all awake.

How busy they are! Work! I should think so!

What a time they have found a place for their homes.

Then they work hard in building them.

Then they must care for their little ones.

How different the big brown house is now from what it was in the winter.

What a busy, buzzing, working, living place it is now.

All the little people are awake, busy and happy at their work.

A COCOON.

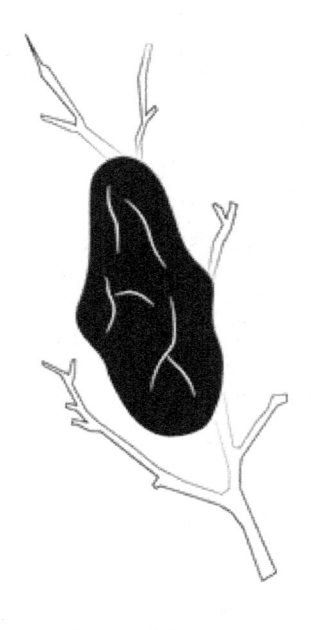

Here is a cocoon.

It is fastened to a little brown twig.

We cannot see inside of it.

We cannot hear anything.

It seems like a poor dead thing.

See what a thick warm covering it has.

No cold can get in to harm the little sleeper inside.

Do you not wonder what is going on inside this little brown house?

A great caterpillar made this house.

He used to live on the maple tree.

Oh! how he did eat leaves!

One day he began to spin.

He spun and worked till his house was done.

Do you think he knows what is going on now?

I think he must be very fast asleep.

THE MOTH

Ah! here you are, you beautiful moth.

Were you not glad to get out of that close little house?

How could you grow so big in that little place?

Where did you get out of it?

At first, your wings were all wrinkled up.

Now they are straight and strong.

How beautiful they are!

Your coat looks like red and white striped velvet.

Your feelers lock like little ferns.

Did you know yourself when you came out with that fine dress?

Do you remember when you were only a caterpillar?

How glad you must be now to fly instead of having to crawl!

Fly away, pretty moth, and try your beautiful wings.

I do not wish to keep you.

A KINGBIRD.

Do you see me? I am a kingbird.

I am a fighter. I will tell you why I fight.

My mate and I made our nest in a cherry tree.

She is sitting in the nest now.

This is my perch up here at the top of this tree.

I sit here all day. I mean to defend my little mate. No harm shall come to her.

If another bird comes here, I give my shrill cry. Then I fly after him.

Yesterday a woodpecker came to get the cherries.

But I would not have it. Not that I care for cherries.

No, indeed; I eat insects.

But I am not going to have him here bothering my mate.

I flew after him. I pulled out some of his feathers.

He was glad to get away, I can tell you.

I have to be pretty brave to stick to my post all the time.

Sometimes a thunder shower comes up, but I do not mind that much.

I just sit here, even if I do get wet.

A soldier must not run, even if something unpleasant does happen.

I must be brave in defending my little mate.

She is doing her part, sitting on the eggs.

By and by we shall have a house full of the dearest children you ever saw.

THE ROBIN'S SONG.

"Cheer up, cheer up, — cheer, cheer!!"

Oh! pretty robin, what a sweet song you are singing. Is your nest in that tree?

No, indeed. I would not sit here to sing if it were.

I do not wish you to know where my nest is.

You might harm my little wife.

You might take away our home.

We have the dearest home in the world. I am so happy. I love to sit here and sing.

Now, I will tell you a secret if you will be kind.

I sing so that my little mate can hear me, and be happy, too.

I do not wish her to be lonesome.

Our nest is not in this tree.

But it is so near that my little wife can hear me.

Now if you find her, you will not harm her or our lithe home, will you?

She does not look just like me.

If she wore such a gay dress as mine, you could find her easily.

So could the cat or any other enemy of ours.

She wears a dress that is suited to what she has to do.

She has to sit on her nest for a long time.

So her dress is nearly the color of the nest and the tree.

You cannot see her easily.

Well, good-by, I must go to find her something to eat.

AN ANT'S STORY.

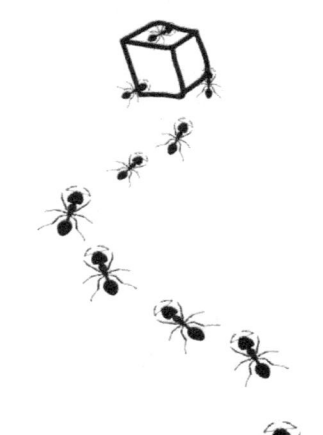

I am a worker ant.

One day I was out hunting something to eat. Soon I found a big piece of sugar,— many times as big as I am.

I wondered where it came from.

I looked up and found that a big giant had brought it to me.

You do not call her a giant. You call her a little girl.

"Well," I thought, "not all these big people are cruel."

I should like to have people study us that way.

She helped us instead of hurting us.

I wished to carry that sugar home, but it was too heavy.

I could barely move it.

So I went to tell another worker about it.

He came to help me.

The little girl said:

"How did that other ant know about this sugar?"

I could not tell her that I told him.

She would not have heard me. She cannot hear the sounds I make.

My friend and I together could not carry the big piece of sugar.

We bit off pieces and carried them home.

At last, we carried them all in.

That little girl wished to learn about us, I am sure.

She had a glass with her.

It made us look bigger, she said.

Her eyes cannot see such little things as we are, very well.

I was glad to let her see how we managed to get into the good store she gave us.

I should like to tell the little girl about the way we live, for she was kind to us.

If she were not so big, I would invite her down into our home.

I would show her all the rooms and halls deep down in the

ground.

Down there is our queen. She is the mother of all.

Once she had wings.

But when she settled down at home she took them off. She did not need them anymore.

She lays the eggs. Then the nurse ants take care of them.

Tiny white grubs come out of these eggs.

A grub looks like a wee white worm.

The nurse ants must feed it and wash it.

They take care of it as if it were a baby.

By and by it goes to sleep in a white case.

You have often been these white bundles.

The nurse ants carry them off if any danger comes near our home.

After a while, the cases open, and full-grown ants come out.

We are very busy, hard-working little people.

I cannot take that little girl down into my home.

I cannot show her the things I have told you about.

But I can take her with me when I go to milk.

She may follow me someday to the primrose bush.

Then she will see where we keep our cows.

She will find many of us running up and down the stem of that plant. It is our cow pasture.

Our cows do not run about as big cows do.

They fasten themselves to the plant, and keep sucking out the sap.

But they take more than they need.

They give it out through two little tubes on their backs.

We call it honey-dew, and are very fond of it.

We pat them gently with our feelers, to get them to give it to us.

One day a dreadful thing happened to some of our cows.

A big red and black monster walked right into our pasture. He ate up some of our cows.

Presently he spread out his coat and flew away.

I heard a little boy say, "O, there goes a Lady Bug!"

We do not give him such a pretty name as that.

We do not like him.

But I am a worker ant, and must not step longer.

Perhaps you may see the little girl who was so kind to us.

Tell her to come on with her glass and sugar whenever she likes.

We shall be glad to let her see all she can.

THE BEST JUMPER.

"I can jump farther than you."

"No, you cannot. I can jump the farthest."

Did you ever hear boys talk that way?

Then you may have seen them try to see which could do best.

Perhaps they Jumped six feet.

You thought they did very well.

I will tell you about the best jumper of all.

His name is Mr. Flea.

What an odd-looking insect!

See, what strong legs!

His body is covered with plates of hard, tough skin.

O, you have seen him, and you do not like him!

Neither do I; but that is no reason why I should not learn something about him.

There is one thing he can do better than any one else.

He can jump two hundred times his own length.

His long hind legs help him to do that.

Think what a spring he must make to go so far!

If a little boy could jump like that, he could go more than a square at one leap.

Would not that be fun?

Well, Mr. Flea, I hope you will use your big jumps to take

yourself away from us.

Then we will not bother you.

A MAY FLY.

Here is a beautiful little May Fly.

Sometimes she is called a Day Fly.

She has but one day to live and enjoy her beautiful wings.

You must not think that is all of her life.

She lived two or three years in the water.

She came out of an egg which her mother left on the water.

Her wings grew while she lived in the water.

Of course, they were kept shut up tight in a case.

She was getting ready for this beautiful day in the air.

By and by she was all ready.

She crept out of the water, and out of her old dress.

And here she is, as dainty and pretty as can be.

Do you feel sorry that she cannot live longer?

She does not need to live more than a day.

She has but one thing to do; she must lay her eggs on the water.

Then her life work is done.

Suppose you or I had to make something that was to last but one day.

Would we try to make it as pretty and perfect as this little May Fly is?

SOME LITTLE HELPERS.

Ah! Here is a poor little dead bird.

It ought not to be left lying here.

Someone ought to bury it.

Look! There are some little people about it.

They are called sexton beetles.

What can they be doing?

I think they are burying the Little bird.

Dig, dig, dig, — how busily they work!

They are digging the dirt out from under it.

So, little by little, the bird sinks down into the ground.

Why do they take all this trouble?

Do they know that the bird's body should not be left lying there?

Perhaps they do not know that.

But they do know that this body is just the food that their little ones will need.

So they are going to leave their eggs there.

And now they are covering it up.

They are doing good, even if they do not know it.

They are helping to keep the earth clean and the air pure.

So while they are at their own work they are doing much good.

Who planned that this should be so?

TUMBLE BUGS.

See those two big fellows with their ball.

What are they doing?

See them rolling, pushing, and tugging with all their might.

Now they are getting on very well.

See! they have come to a high place.

How can they get up?

Push and tug!—there! they are almost to the top.

Ah! a slip, —down they go, bugs and ball to the foot of the hill.

It looks very funny.

Do they give up their hard task?

They get up and try again.

I feel almost as if I should like to help them.

But perhaps they would not thank me.

Ah! now they are up the hill.

Down they go, rolling over and over, on the other side.

Up again and at their work.

What does this mean?

Where did they get the ball?

What are they going to do with it?

They made it themselves.

They have put an egg inside of If.

This ball is made of just what their baby will need to eat.

Now they are going to take the ball to a safe place.

Perhaps they will take it to the side of the road.

If you watch them, you will see them cover it up.

Then they will go away satisfied.

They have done their part.

They have provided for their little ones.

A LITTLE CARPENTER.

"What are you doing, little bee?

"Are you getting ready to make a house?

"Do you mean to have that tree cut down and hauled away?"

"I am hunting a place to make a house.

"This twig suits me pretty well.

"But I shall not need to cut it down and take it away.

"I come right here where the wood grows, to build my house."

"So you are a carpenter. I do not see your tools. How can

you make a house without tools?"

"I carry my tools with me. I can bore down into this twig.

"That is the way I make my little round front hall.

"Then I make little rooms down the middle of the twig.

"I put walls between the rooms. The walls are made from chippings that come from boring the hole.

"I stick them together with a glue of my own making.

"Each room that I make is to be the home tor one baby bee.

"It is a great deal of work to make such a house as mine.

"But I am making it for my little children, so I work very gladly."

"You are a pretty fine little carpenter, I think.

"Do you make any new style houses?

"Do you try to make them any better than bees used to make?

"The carpenters that I know, make better and finer houses than carpenters used to make.

"Perhaps you cannot learn to do that. But 1 am sure you do the best you can."

A QUEER FELLOW.

His name is Walking Stick.

That is a queer name, is it not?

He is a queer fellow, too.

His name tells just what he is like.

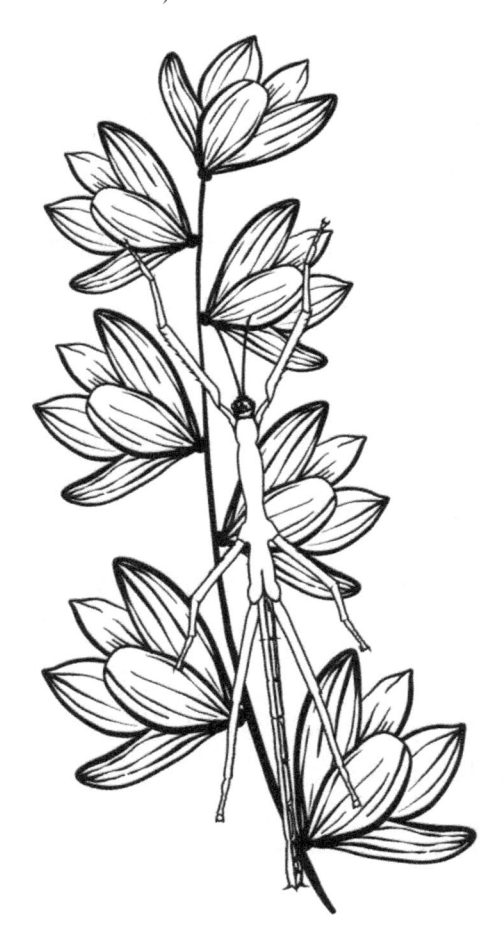

See! He looks almost like a stick, or twig.

You would scarcely see him as he sits there upon the twig.

He is just about the color and shape of a little twig.

But he really has a head and legs.

When he walks, he looks very much like a stick walking. So he has a name that fits him pretty well.

Can you think why he has such a queer shape?

He cannot be easily seen as he is.

His queer shape helps protect him from harm.

Even this humble little insect has a way given him to protect himself.

His Maker gave him what he most needed.

A LADY BUG'S TALK.

Of course, you all know me.

My name is Lady Bug.

Sometimes I am called Lady Bird.

See my beautiful red and black cloak!

I have a pair of wings folded up safe under it.

Did you not know that I can fly?

Watch me some time and see.

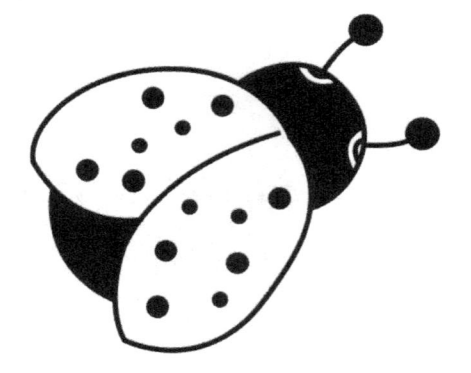

Do you know what I do sometimes when I am scared?

I drop down suddenly and lie quite still.

I draw up my legs and try to look as if I were dead.

I think no one will harm me if he thinks me already dead.

When my enemy is gone, I can fly away.

Did you know that I am your friend?

I never do you any harm.

Indeed, I do you much good.

You shall be glad to see me.

You have seen little green bugs on some plants,

Of course, you do not like to have them there.

They harm the plants.

They are the very things that my friends and I like best for food.

So we take off as many as we can.

The more Lady Birds there are, the fewer green bugs on the plants.

My children like these green bugs, too.

So I always leave my little yellow eggs where there is plenty of food.

When the little ones creep out, they need not go far to find their dinner.

They are very, very greedy little ones.

But they are growing fast, you see; so they must eat a great deal.

My children do not look at all like me when they are little.

They are dark-colored grubs with yellow spots.

They have no wings.

They must sleep for a time in a little case glued to the underside of a leaf.

Then they come out LadyBirds like me.

Do not forget that I am your friend.

Be a friend to me.

A LITTLE ACTOR.

One day I walked in the meadow.

All at once, there was a little quail fluttering along in front of me.

I could not see where it came from.

"Poor little thing," I said, "how lame you are!

"You must be badly hurt.

"I will pick you up and see what I can do for you."

But I did not pick her up.

Just as I got to her, she flew away as well as could be.

What could she mean by "playing hurt" in that way?

She saw me coming near her and her little ones.

Perhaps she thought: "I will make that person think I am lame.

"I will limp and flutter away from here.

"When I get her far enough away from my little ones, I will fly away."

You poor little mother! How hard you tried to protect your

little ones!

You took a pretty good way, too.

For surely I never thought of your children, but only of you.

But you need not have feared me.

I would not hurt your babies.

A LITTLE GYMNAST.

Do you know who this is? It is Mr. Looper.

He makes his body into a loop as he walks.

Is not that a queer way of walking?

Do you know why he must walk that way?

He has no legs in the middle part of his body.

If he wishes his back legs to come up with his front ones, he must make a loop of himself.

Watch him some time to see how he does it.

Sometimes he wishes to go from a tree to the ground.

He has a cute way of doing that.

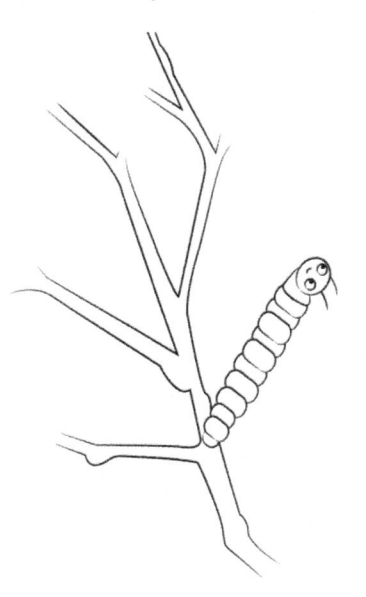

He swings himself down by a silken thread.

He spins it himself as he goes.

He can climb back up his thread if he likes.

But I must tell you what a hard thing he can do.

He can hold himself to a twig with his two back legs.

Then he can stretch his body out free from the twig.

He can remain straight and still that way for a long time.

Do you not think that is a hard exercise?

He looks almost exactly like a twig when he does that.

Can you think why he does such a thing?

Perhaps he thinks the birds will suppose he is only a twig and let him alone.

Is it not wonderful that even a measuring worm has a way to protect himself?

A LIVING LIGHT.

Here is a little fairy who flies about in the night.

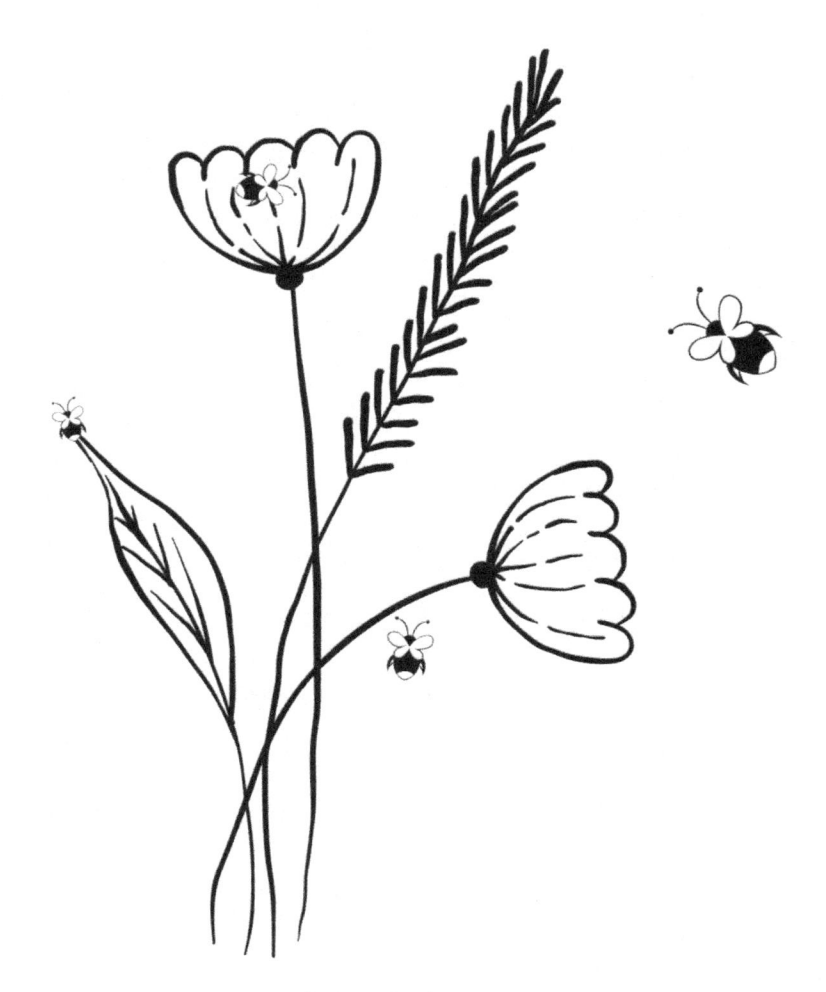

But he does not mind the dark.

Indeed, why should he?

He carries his own little light with him.

You have often seen him with his little candle.

You call him a Firefly.

Did you ever think what a queer fire he has?

It does not burn him.

It will not feel warm to you if you hold your hand near him.

Yet what a bright little spark he carries!

How beautiful it looks to see these little earth-stars flying about at night!

Mr. Firefly is a very plain little body in the day.

With his sober dress we would scarcely see him among so many bright-colored flowers and butterflies.

But at night we cannot see them.

Then he comes out and does his part to make the world bright.

A LITTLE MESSENGER.

Here is a fine little messenger.

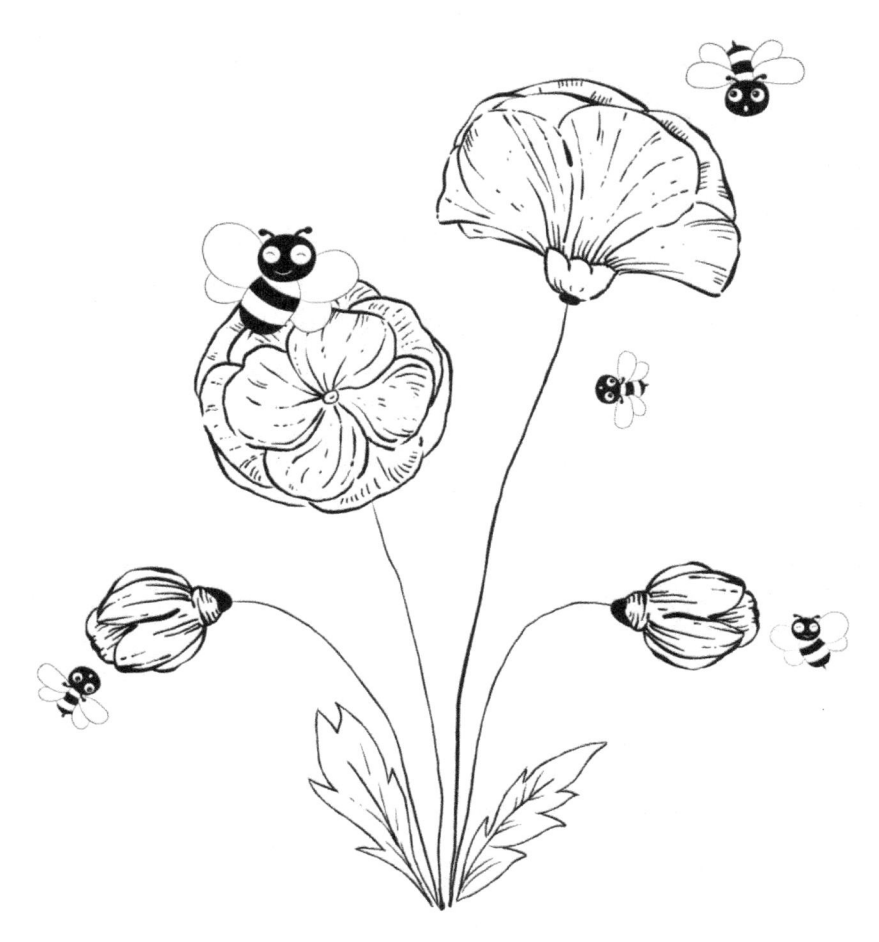

He is dressed in velvet and gold.

He is a pretty noisy little fellow.

"Hum, hum, buzz, buzz," all day.

He is a very faithful messenger.

You must not bother him about his work.

Perhaps he may fight you if you do.

He goes to see Red Clover.

"Good morning, dear Clover," he says. "I have brought you something nice.

"Here is some flower-dust from your friend across the field."

"Thank you, Mr. Beo," says Red Clover.

"How glad I am to get it!

"I was needing some flower-dust very much.

"I use il to make my seeds grow.

"Will you go back to my friend and take her some of my Nower-dust?

"That will help her seeds to grow."

"That I will," says Mr. Bumble Bee.

And so all day this little messenger flies about from flower to flower.

He carries a good message to each one.

But who pays him for all his trouble?

Does he get nothing for himself?

Oh, yes, indeed! the pretty red clovers pay him.

Such sweet honey as they have for him!

No one knows how to get it so well as he.

His cousin Honey Bee, cannot get it at all.

Perhaps the red clovers like him better than any other messenger.

I am glad, Mr. Buinble Bee, that you are such a good messenger.

I am glad the red clovers pay you well with their sweet honey.

I fear we would have no red clover if it were not for you.

A LITTLE GARDENER.

This gardener is a little earthworm.

He is not pretty to look at.

He has no legs. He has no eyes.

He does not look much like a gardener.

Perhaps we think he is of no use.

He may not seem to us worth thinking about.

But still, he is a most wonderful little worker.

He and his friends are of much use in the world.

They keep the earth loose about the roots of plants.

Sometimes they have made a rough stony field good to use.

How do such humble little things do so much?

How can they cover a field with rich dirt?

They have no spades to dig with.

They have no baskets nor wagons to carry up the soil.

So they make baskets for themselves.

They fill their own bodies full of the soil.

Then they carry it up and leave little casts of themselves on the ground.

Of course one of these little gardeners cannot do much.

But there are so many of them.

Then they work, work, work so steadily.

Each one does his own little part.

And by and by a great good thing is done.

A HUMMING BIRD.

See this dear little bird.

Watch her dart from flower to flower.

See her put her long slender bill into the flowers.

What holds her up in the air?

Her wings are moving so fast that they keep her up.

Have you ever seen her at rest?

She is a very shy little bird.

Sometimes she makes her nest on the limb of a tree,

She covers it on the outside with mess or lichens,

It looks almost like a knot on the limb.

On the inside, she makes her neat very soft.

She lays two very tiny white eggs in the nest.

It is very hard to find her nest.

She tries as hard as she can to keep it from being found.

See what beautiful colors she wears!

She looks almost like a flower herself.

You can scarcely see her when she is among the flowers.

Perhaps she wears such a gay dress that she may not be easily seen.

We are glad to have you come to our flowers, little bird.

We will not do you any harm.

A HAWK MOTH.

What is this flying about over the flowers?

Is it a humming bird?

It looks a little like one.

If he would only stop, we would soon see that he is not a bird.

He has six legs and four wings, instead of two legs and two wings.

He has no beak like a bird.

Instead of that, he has a very long tongue, like a hair.

He can unroll it, until it is several inches long.

He uses it to reach down into the flowers that have long tubes.

He is as dainty about his food as a humming bird.

He was not always so dainty as he is now.

He began life on a tomato vine.

He was called a tobacco worm, or a tomato worm.

He was very greedy then.

He had a very queer little way of raising his head. Perhaps you have seen him do it.

He went into the ground for his long nap.

So he did not need to make a thick cocoon to keep him warm in winter.

He slept in a queer little case down in the ground.

There was a little stem on one side of his case.

Perhaps his long tongue was stored away there.

When spring came he crept out of his dark bed.

He went forth to feed upon the flowers.

Next time you see a tomato worm, perhaps you will feel more interest in him.

Now you know his story. You know what a pretty winged thing he may become.

A SNAIL.

"How do you do, Mr. Snail?

"Where are you going?

"I do not think you will get there very soon.

"You go so slowly.

"I know now what people mean when they say 'as slow as a snail.'

"Why do you go so slowly?"

"Look what I have on my back. It is my house.

"Suppose you had to carry your house with you, should you not go slowly?"

"Why do you not leave your house in one place and go back to it as I do?"

"I could not do that. I need to have it with me.

"If I went without it, my soft body might easily be hurt.

"So you see I carry my house with me. When there is any

danger I can creep inside of it."

"So you cannot run from any danger?"

"No, indeed; I have but one foot. I could not run at all.

"But I do not need to run home as you do.

"My home is always with me, you see"

"Well, for my part, I do not see how you get about at all.

"Just think of having a house to carry and only one foot to walk with!"

"I cannot go very fast, as you see; but I do my best.

"When I start, I keep at it.

"So I can really go farther than you think."

A DRAGON.

Do you see me?

See my four beautiful wings!

See my big bright eyes!

Some little children call me a snake feeder.

That is not my name.

I have nothing to do with snakes.

I am a Dragon Fly. I am a dragon to little insects.

But you need not be afraid of me. I will not hurt you. Indeed, I do you much good.

I like insects for my dinner. Of course, you are glad to have me take them out of your way.

You should see how many mosquitoes I catch.

I sit very still and watch sharply till I see one. All at once, I dart at him very swiftly. He cannot get away.

You see I like to stay near the water.

It was my old home. Do I look as I ever lived in the water?

I had no wings then, you may be sure.

My food was little water insects.

I wore a mask over my face. Then the insects could not see my strong jaws.

I could swim up and catch them.

I lived in the water for some time.

My beautiful wings were growing under my old skin.

At last, I knew I was ready to leave my old home. So I crept up along lily stem.

My old coat split open and I crept out.

Then I had to wait for my wings to spread out and grow strong.

How glad I was to be out in the bright sunshine!

I can fly back and forth very swiftly through the air.

Ah! there is a big mosquito!

He will never trouble you.

See how swiftly I will dart after him.

A CAREFUL LITTLE MOTHER.

Here is one of the queerest of insect mothers.

She is not liked very well. She has not a pretty name, either. She is called an earwig.

Perhaps you may find her sometime under a stone.

She has queer little wings.

They fold up like a fan. Then she doubles them crosswise and puts them under her wing cases.

But I must tell you what kind of a little mother she is.

We have read of some insect mothers who never see their babies.

But I assure you she does.

She really sits on her eggs like a mother hen.

When the little ones hatch out, she leads them about to find food.

She takes very good care of them.

Is it not queer there are so many different ways these little folks have of caring for their children?

There is always something new and interesting for us to learn.

It is never possible for us to know it all.

THE MOST WONDERFUL OF ALL.

I.

I have told you some stories of some little beings about us.

We have read many queer things about them and their babies.

Many of these babies know at once how to take care of themselves.

Some of them make houses to live in.

Some make themselves cases or dresses.

They know how to make these bigger when they are too small.

They know what kind of food they need.

They know where and how to get it.

Many of them know how to spin a cocoon for themselves.

They seem to know they must go into it for a long sleep.

They finally grow to be just like their parents.

They build houses just as their parents did and no better.

They take care of their little ones just as they were taken care of.

They eat the same kind of food.

They have the same kind of tools given them.

They use them in the same way.

They run or fly, or crawl or walk just as their parents did.

II.

Now let us hear about the most wonderful baby of all.

He cannot take care of himself.

He cannot make his own clothes nor find his own food. He cannot make himself a house to live in.

His parents do all these things for him. He cannot fly or swim nor run.

He cannot even walk till he learns how.

I do not need to tell you what kind of a baby this is. You know already.

Perhaps you have one in your own house.

You know that he will be a man when he is grown.

He is not wonderful for what he can do now. But the wonderful part is what he may learn to do.

III.

Let us think of some of the wonderful things a man can do.

He cannot fly; but he can make a balloon that will carry bim up through the air.

He cannot run very fast; but he can take cars and an engine. These will carry him much faster than any animal can run.

He cannot swim very well; but he can make a boat that will carry him over the water faster than a fish can swim.

He has no house given to him, as Mr. Snail has; but he can make for himself an excellent house.

He has no coat of feathers nor scales nor fur given him; but he can make beautiful clothes for himself.

He has no light given him to carry about in the dark, as Mr. Firefly has; but he knows where to get gas and make a light.

He knows, too, how to make a light as brilliant as the lightning itself.

He has no saw nor chisel nor drills have given him; but he knows how to make all these things and more for himself.

He has not such wonderful eyes as even a fly; but he knows how to make glasses that will let him see things he could not see at all without them.

One of these glasses makes things look more than a hundred times their real size.

So man can learn about many things in the world that his own eyes could never see.

The other glass helps him to see things far away, like the sun and moon and stars.

It makes them seem nearer; then he can learn about them.

Man cannot hear a sound very far away; but he knows how to make something that will carry sound all around the world in less than a minute.

So he can know what goes on all over the world every day.

He can learn to read what people have said and written down hundreds of years ago.

So he knows what happened in the world long before he came into it.

Does not man seem to you a very wise and wonderful being?

He can be what is better still.

Think how many stories we have read of men who have been brave and strong and true.

How often have they been kind and helpful to people not so strong as they were?

As they do such things they grow more and more like their Maker.

Who taught the spider how to make
Is her silken web so light?
Who gave her such a cunning way
To take her airy flight?

Who told the timid little bird?
To play that she was lame,
And try to lead me far away
When near her young I came?

Who taught a little mother wasp?
To make her paper nest,
And work away the summer hours
Without a thought of rest?

How does a little honey bee
Know how to make her cell,
And fill it with such dainty food
To feed her babies well?

It was their Maker gave to them

Such wondrous skillful ways;

He gives them all some work to do

Through all the summer days.

He gives to us, my children dear,

More skill of mind and heart;

Then surely we should try our best

To do our part as well.

OTHER BOOKS FROM THE PUBLISHER

I. Natures Stories For Young Readers: Plant Life (Illustrated)

Author: Florence Bass

The children should observe the plants in the different stages of growth indicated, when reading the lessons descriptive of those stages.

Such a lesson as **"Spring Rain"** will be best appreciated by the children if read on just such a day as it describes.

Many of the lessons aim to give only a particular instance of a general truth, to lead the children to discover for themselves other like instances, and finally infer the truth itself: for example, **"The Chestnut Burr"** will lead to a discussion of the different ways in which seeds are protected until they are ripe; **"The Beech Nuts,"** to the storing up of food in the seed, which the young plant will need when it begins to grow; **"The Milkweed,"** to the various ways in which seeds are scattered; **"The Jamestown Weed,"** to the mutual help of insects and plants, and so on.

It has not seemed amiss to let the children see that there is something beautiful and interesting even in the most common and despised weeds.

Pick it up to enjoy endless time together with your children!

https://www.amazon.com/dp/B09BY815Z9

II. The Vintage Mother Goose Nursery Rhymes Book: A Beautiful Collection of Favorite Nursery Rhymes (Illustrated)

Rediscover 80+ Timeless Nursery Rhymes of Mother Goose in This Colorful Illustrated Book!

- Children and adults will be delighted by this freshly presented collection of classic nursery rhymes that includes all your childhood favorites:
- A nursery rhymes book that's a great addition to a child's bookshelf.
- A book that's perfect for a baby gift, a baby shower, or a grandparent, and other special occasions: Christmas, Easter, Valentine's Day, birthdays, and more!

Pick it up to enjoy endless time together with your toddler!

https://www.amazon.com/dp/B09K1LTMZH

III. Rhythmic Games and Dances for Children (Illustrated)

Author: Florence Krik

Play With Your Kids: 52 Traditional Games and Exercises, 50+ Classic Songs For Children (with Illustrations, Sheet Music, and Lyrics)!

Encourages children to develop their imaginations, social skills, self-expression, and coordination with this collection of Exercises and Games, Old English Games and Dances. Inside Rhythmic Games and Dances for Children, you'll find:

- Exercises and Games for Children under Five♥
- Games without Music♥
- Old English Games and Dances♥
- Swedish Games and Dances♥
- Various Marches and Steps♥

This book gathered the melodies, rules, movements of 50+ games and songs. Lyrics and music melody lines are included for 50+ songs including **"Oranges and Lemons", "Green Grass", "Oats and Beans and Barley", "Hickory, Dickory, Dock", "Garden Game", "The Sleeping Princess"**... These games are still being played in the open air, but also at home if there's room enough.

Pick it up:

https://www.amazon.com/dp/B09BY88JM4

IV. History Through Familiar Things (Part 1 & Part 2)

Author: Joseph Rebekoff Reeve

History Stories from the Dawn of Civilization to the Modern Life Through Familiar Things!

The history of everyday things — a loaf of bread, a knife, a wheel, a house, a ship, your coat — is the exciting story of man's struggle with his surroundings and his ultimate triumph.

There was a time, long, long ago, when there were no houses and no buses, when even bread was unknown, when the few men on the earth's surface did not know whence their next meal was to come, when men, in fact, lived a life little above that of animals. Today we have huge ocean liners, railway trains, powerful machinery, skyscrapers, and a sufficient and varied supply of clothing for a huge world population...

The truth is, that in machines and scientific knowledge we have today the means to a greater civilization than we have ever attained. **Science and machines have brought the peoples of the world closer together, can they find means of living harmoniously together?**

Buy book to learn more:

https://www.amazon.com/dp/B09244XVVD

V. Activity Book For Kids Ages 4-8

Author: Lillian Garda

How To Draw All The Things For Kids (Step-by-Step Drawing):

https://www.amazon.com/dp/B08MH51RZG

VI. Activity Book For Kids Ages 8-14

500+ logic puzzles and brain games for kids to **develop logical reasoning, quick thinking, critical analysis, and creative problem-solving:**

https://www.amazon.com/dp/B08T7L9R61

VII. Other Books

1. Big Book Of Sudoku Hard To Expert For Adults and Kids: 1000+ Hard Sudoku Puzzles

https://www.amazon.com/dp/B08SPKR45J

2. Big Book of Sudoku Easy to Medium For Adults and Kids: 1000+ Easy Sudoku Puzzles

https://www.amazon.com/dp/B08WV25WLV

3. Big Book Of Sudoku Medium To Hard For Adults and Kids: 1000+ Puzzles

https://www.amazon.com/dp/B08SRFB8GX

4. 200+ Large Print Sudoku Puzzles Medium To Hard For Adults and Kids!

https://www.amazon.com/dp/B08RQSLLPY

5. Brain Games Book For Adult

An Activity Book Large Print for Seniors and Adults with easy Sudokus, Cryptograms, Word Searches, Mazes, and More! (With Solutions) - This activity book includes many types of games for your mind: **Sudokus, Word Searches, Mazes, Skyscraper Puzzles, Mines Finder Puzzles, Battleship Puzzles, Cryptograms.** They are becoming wildly popular with people of all ages, especially for seniors and adults to *relax, reduce stresses, improve brain health, and support preventing Alzheimer's disease.*

https://www.amazon.com/dp/B08RZGN5VL

6. Brain Games For The Elderly

Memory games for elderly adults can be not only interesting and entertaining, but can also improve memory, daily life skills, and overall mental health.

210+ Brain Games for Seniors with Memory Problems Large Print (With Solutions):

https://www.amazon.com/dp/B08WZL1VWX

Made in the USA
Monee, IL
09 January 2022